THE LOST
& FOUND
OF LIFE

FINDING THE LIFE
YOU HAVE ALWAYS WANTED

REV. DR. CARMELA NANTON

CARMEL MINISTRIES INTERNATIONAL INC.

Dedication

This book is dedicated to my husband, prayer covering and tireless supporter, my children, and all who are seeking.

Contents

Preface: Why He Came

Jesus is so serious about finding you that He left his home in heaven, traveling trillions of light years to earth. God, taking on humanities' physical limitations, manifest in Jesus Christ who gave his very life on the cross of Calvary, entered life as we know it to make it easy for you to find him. As easy as accepting a gift! Your heart will eternally seek the breadth, the depth of meaning and height of contentment in life until you find your rest and peace in him. You need not stay in the "lost and found" of your life for another moment!

"For the Son of man came to seek and save those who are lost." Luke 19:10 (NLT).

The Hound of Heaven

How little worthy of any love thou art!
Whom wilt thou find to love ignoble thee
Save Me, save only Me?
All which I took from thee I did but take, Not for thy
harms.
But just that thou might'st seek it in my arms.
All which thy child's mistake
Fancies as lost, I have stored for thee at home; Rise, clasp
My hand, and come!"
Halts by me that footfall;
Is my gloom, after all,
Shade of His hand, outstreched caressingly?
"Ah, fondest, blindest, weakest,
I am He Whom thou seekest!
Thou dravest love from thee, who dravest Me."

Francis Thompson (1893)[1]

Introduction

This excerpt from Francis Thompson's poem[1] captures central concepts of this book. It is, in fact, the best part. It is the part that confirms that Jesus loves us enough to pursue us, to stay close enough to us so that when we finally turn to Him, we discover that He has been right there all the time. In essence, our nature is to run from God, the very one through whom we live, move and have our being. We need Him, but we run from Him. This odd trend is the result of sin in our lives which tends to drive us from the very one who can set us at peace. This book captures the reality of feeling lost and ungrounded in life until we have been found by the One who satisfies us and makes us whole and complete. This metaphor for living is illustrated by the Lost and Found concept.

CHAPTER 1

The Lost and Found

HAVE YOU EVER needed to go to the Lost and Found? Or wished that there *was* a Lost and Found when you could not find an item that you had misplaced? Even if you have never used the Lost and Found, or even if you have never referred someone to it, you probably know its vital purpose.

Anywhere there are children, whether on playgrounds, schools, or community centers, the Lost and Found is needed. Children tend to lose things: sometimes very important things. But losing things is not unique to children. Many adults also have the tendency to misplace things. Once misplaced, the owner of the lost item goes to the Lost and Found first to reclaim his or her property. Hopefully, the owner can do so before someone else does. Some people are *always* at the Lost and Found because they are careless, unorganized, or simply don't pay close attention to their things so they lose them or misplace them. Other people are rarely at the Lost and Found, except perhaps to find things for themselves that others have not claimed or reclaimed.

Owners Missing in Action

If the owners of the items in question do not return for them, the items remain at the Lost and Found until they are thrown away, given away or redeemed by someone else. These owners are "missing in action." The items are waiting to be redeemed, but the owner is not around to redeem them. Like people in similar positions, these items may feel they are of no value because they are not important enough to be claimed by their owners. At first, there may be hope that the owner will show up; but as time goes by, that hope begins to fade as the other items around them are redeemed and they are left behind. The interesting thing about this is that the owner can also be *looking* for that item, turning over everything trying to remember where it may have been lost, trying to recall the last place it was used, wondering whether it will ever be found again.

How awful it must be to be left unclaimed by the owner! To be forgotten or replaced by the one to whom you belong, never to be reclaimed by the owner. This idea has stuck with me for a while in relation to life because there are people wandering through life as if they are living in the Lost and Found. They have no sense of purpose, no feeling of belonging, and they eventually begin to detect a growing feeling of abandonment. Living in the Lost and Found in life can have some dire and eternal consequences, but one does not have to permanently live in a state of abandonment. There is a God who is looking for each of us, and who, like the hound of heaven, will continue to follow us, seeking to be reconciled with us to the original loving relationship that we could have had before sin entered into the world.

He, the Lord Jesus, is looking for us so that we do not have to remain unclaimed and forgotten any longer, and He stays close enough to us that we don't even have to be claimed by others at all. He will make certain that every person knows they have an owner: a Redeemer. He ensures that the number of lost persons (or the pile of lost possessions in the Lost and Found) does not get bigger than it needs to be. Anyone who is willing can be claimed by their owner, or they can see the owner and can claim Him. Here's where the metaphor changes in a powerful and important way. Lost and found items are inanimate objects that must wait for the owner to claim them, but people who live in the Lost and Found of life don't have to wait for their Owner-Redeemer to find them - they can also seek out the Owner on their own! When the seeker finds the sought, and the Redeemer claims the bought, the wanderer finds the right path, and the dying find new life.

This book takes the metaphor of the Lost and Found and applies it to the journey of our lives, connecting it to the concepts of life in the world as the 'Lost and Found' of life; where we are lost and waiting for someone to come to find or reclaim us; taking us out of that lonely and confusing place to put us on the path to a life worth living. When we are found and reclaimed, we are brought home to the "fold" to be nurtured and taken care of. Yes, I did say "fold" because the other related and vital point for us to take away from this book is the example of sheep that God uses liberally in his Word. He did this to aid us in our understanding of what can and will happen to us in our lives if we are not connected to God in the original, completely satisfying relationship he planned for us before the foundation of the earth.

Reflection

1. Have you thought about what it means to have God, creator of the universe actively seeking you out, longing to find you?
2. Do you believe that seeking God is a mutual affair? You are seeking him and he is seeking you?

Prayer

Lord, I thank you for coming this far to seek me out. As you seek me, help me to find in you all I need. Amen

CHAPTER 2

Like a Shepherd

THE CLEAREST AND most frequent animal God compares human beings to is sheep. God does that because sheep resemble humans in their behavior and, as we will soon see, in their characteristics. Let us then first look at some of the characteristics that might be strikingly similar to our human tendencies. There are some interesting comparisons for us to consider.

Dependence on God

Sheep are dependent: helpless in terms of protecting themselves. They cannot defend themselves except to run: they have no claws, armor, teeth, venom nor any other built in protective mechanisms. Though some of them have horns, they do not use them for self-protection. Human beings are unable to protect themselves on many levels even though we have several mechanisms for self-protection, such as our fists, weapons, and locks. Yet, when we consider it, we are quite often unable to prevent burglaries; when fires, hurricanes or tornadoes arise, we are often reduced to running and hiding from them for our very survival.

Total Dependence

Our human helplessness and presence in life's Lost and Found is described in Psalms 23, one of the most well-known Scriptures, where God and his loving care over us are directly highlighted in the analogy of the shepherd and sheep relationship. The author David would understand such a relationship because he had experience as a shepherd caring for his own sheep. We will look at this specifically in the chapter on what happens when we find Jesus.

As human beings, we are totally dependent on God for some of the most vital aspects of our lives. Three things that we call involuntary (that happen outside our control) and which are essential to us staying alive highlight our dependency on God. So dependent in fact, that we need God for every breath, for each heartbeat, and even for each blink of our eyelids. Without these essential functions, we would not live for very long or be able to see. Each of these is critical for us to live, but none of them are within our actual control.

All we like Sheep

Now, looking at it from the sheep's perspective, we can draw some important parallels between people's lives and the lives of sheep. I am so thankful that we have a Shepherd who cares so much for our every need! The purpose of his caring is our contentment and peace throughout our lives. All that God provides for us as his sheep

– from the food and water to the comfort and protection of his rod, staff, and oil – they are all designed to make sure that our needs are continually met, no matter what we are going through or where life's journey takes us. In His presence is blessing and satisfaction, as David later points out in Psalm 34:8: *Oh taste and see that the LORD is good. Blessed is the man that trusts in him!* (NKJV).

Exercising the Will to Choose

Sheep have a tendency to stubbornness, going their own way or wandering off and getting lost. Does this sound familiar? One of the blessings that God has given us that distinguishes us from animals is free will. He gave us the ability to choose right from wrong. But this very blessing has turned out to be a major problem for some of us. Why? Because, like sheep, we also need guidance in our decision making. People can be quite stubborn, wanting things our own way.

Like sheep, people tend to travel in flocks. We group together with others of like minds or similar interests because we want to belong. These can range from professional groups to associations, churches, communities, cliques, or gangs, depending on our inclination. Membership in these groups can become a problem when we exclude others from that group or discriminate against others who are not a part of the group. If the group takes on a mob mentality or engages in detrimental behavior, it can be a source of many problems.

Sheep are also fearful animals, so they have a strong tendency to scatter in many directions. They need a shepherd to keep them together. They can also act quite senseless, may not even recognize when they are in danger, and they are needy. They need someone to protect them – they cannot save themselves.

Out of Balance

One of the most interesting facts I found in my research on sheep is that sheep can fall, lose their balance, or be pushed over if they have too much wool or are pregnant. Once they have fallen over, they cannot get up on their own, but will die if they are not turned over in a short space of time.

When I learned this, it stood out to me because of how people can also get thrown off balance by life's circumstances and accidents, especially if they are at a place of weakness or are working towards birthing a vision that God gave them. They can easily remain out of balance, and can even die if they are not rescued by the Lord.

In those times, the shepherd needs to step in and help them turn things around again. To literally lift them up, hold them until the strength or energy returns to their lives and they are again in balance, able to walk on their own. Have you ever been in such a place or position, when life events knock you off your feet? At such times we need a gentle, firm, but understanding touch from the hand of God. This leads us to why God was so upset with the Shepherds in Ezekiel 34.

Shirking Responsibility

In Ezekiel 34, we see that God has serious expectations

in relations to those who are appointed as shepherds. In that passage, the shepherds took care of themselves and did not focus on the needs of the sheep. Not only that, but we are told that the shepherds dealt forcefully with the sheep, not protecting them, but abusing them. Even knowing they were vulnerable, weak and needy, the shepherds did not look out for the sheep's safety or take care of them; when the sheep wandered away, the shepherds did not go after them. They failed to seek the sheep out when they went missing.

God was upset with the shepherds and He condemned them for their lack of shepherding. So God, unsatisfied, decided that He was going to take over for them and do it the way He wanted it to be done. Not only that, but He specified that He would hold them accountable for the sheep that they failed to bring in, failed to protect, failed to correct, failed to nurture and to care for. Why? Because the sheep need such care – they are dependent on the Shepherd for their very survival.

Responsibility to care

God then moves from rebuking the shepherds to addressing other stronger sheep in the fold. There were some that treated other, weaker sheep harshly; they would push them around, eat their food or trample on it, drink their water or pollute it, making their lives difficult. God says that He will judge between sheep; by that He means the strong will be held accountable for how they treated the weaker ones.

The fundamental question: is it really the responsibility

of strong sheep to bear the infirmities of the weak? The Scripture says yes! Galatians 6:2 says, *"Bear one another's burdens and so fulfill the law of Christ."* There is a responsibility for both the shepherd and the strong to care for others throughout the flock – especially the lambs, especially the weak ones.

The wolf, or the enemy, will not come after the older, stronger sheep first. The enemy will go after the lambs, the weaker ones, causing them to turn away, to wander off. Or the enemy will destroy them or separate them from the others. And when they are alone outside, defenseless, they are vulnerable to death and destruction, to being lost and alone.

The result of this mistreatment in Ezekiel is that the sheep were scattered in several different directions. And going in their own direction, they ended up in sinful lives that eventually led to their destruction. God was definitely not happy with this because these shepherds had abdicated their responsibility to care for the sheep. They had left the sheep to fend for themselves. And since the shepherds were not morally and ethically up to task, they abandoned their required lifestyle and began a journey that took them away from God.

Reflection

1. Think of all the things a shepherd does for the sheep. Which of them are you most in need of?
2. Where has your life been out of balance? Are there 'shepherds' in your life to help you get back on your feet?

Prayer

Lord, thank you that you are the good shepherd. Help me to know that trusting and depending on you in my weakness, allows your strength to be made perfect. Amen.

CHAPTER 3

Journey Away From God

WHY WOULD GOD spend 40 years preparing Moses with sheep? Why did Joseph and David both spend the early years of their lives tending sheep? What did these three legendary men have in common? They became leaders!

Isaiah 53:6 says *all we like sheep who have gone astray* (or really, we are lost) *we have turned everyone to his own way* (doing what we want to do, when we want to do it) *and the Lord has laid on him the iniquity of us all."* (ESV).

From the time Adam and Eve sinned in the Garden, the tendency and desire to meet with God in the Garden and fellowship with Him has changed to a tendency to hide from Him: a tendency, as the Scripture illustrates, to run *from* Him in an attempt to get our own way. However, a deep-rooted desire to connect with God remains with us eternally. It is sustained and fueled by God's personal desire for us to fellowship with Him through the spirit He placed in us along with the spiritual connection (and hunger) He created in us for Himself. This is a space that only He can fill. So his hunger for fellowship matches our hunger for Him, but God knew up front that some of us would not desire Him.

Here's how God puts it in Isaiah 65: 1-3 "*I revealed myself to those who did not ask for me, I was found by those that did not call on my name. I said here am I; Here am I. All day long I have held out my hands to an obstinate people. Who walk in ways not good, pursuing their own imaginations- a people who continually provoke me to my very face,…*" He is saying: Here I am ready to be asked for things by those who will not ask, I am ready to be sought out by those who did not seek me and to be found by those who are not even looking to find me – what an awful position to be in. He is looking for us so He can bring us into the fold and protect us. He is looking to take care of our needs, to satisfy us, to guide us, and shape us so we can have all He created us to have. These are the very things we are seeking to find on our own. How ironic that these two complementary, lock and key relational needs may never meet! Instead of the magnetic attraction that would normally occur, the sin in the midst serves as a repelling force with potential to separate us from our fellowship with God.

Jesus is seeking out those who don't even seek Him, love Him or ask for Him. He is calling out "here I am," yet many of us are going the other way – our own way. Where does such behavior come from? I would remind you that when God created man, He also "breathed into his nostrils the breath of life and *man became a living soul"* (Genesis 2:7).

This means that there is a God-breathed space in us, a place in us that belongs to and is satisfied by God's Spirit alone. But when sin came into the world, all of us born of a man and a woman were automatically endowed with a sinful nature. That sinful nature is what causes us to want to run *away* from God. It is this space that many people go around trying to fill - but because we are moving *away* from God and not *to* God, we end up doing wrong things, going wrong places, not understanding even why we are doing what we are doing. Some of us are confused, going around from state to state, from job to job, and from lover to lover, seeking that which we know not: continuously seeking yet always unsatisfied.

The Fight Within

We are actually in a conflicted and confusing position, where on the one hand our sin nature causes us to move away from God, while on the other hand we have a built-in need that draws us to God. We are pulled in both directions at the same time. For some people, this can result in devastating outcomes. Some cannot still the voices in their heads or the voices from their friends, parents, or enemies that play like broken records over and over. More specifically, we end up doing what we know we should not be doing, and we are not able to stop ourselves. Paul puts it this way when he admits to his own struggles in Romans 7: 21, *"When I would do good, evil is present with me."*[2] By the time he gets to the end of the chapter, he is so torn and pulled in different directions between what he should be doing and what he actually was doing that he finally cried out, "*Oh wretched man that I am –Who will deliver me from this body?*" I am so thankful that he did not leave it there, but answers his own question at the end of the chapter and into Chapter 8 by saying, "*Thanks be unto God through Jesus Christ our Lord... There is therefore now no condemnation to those who are in Christ Jesus!*" What an awesomely freeing response to the confusion and struggle Paul described. If you are struggling like Paul was, doing things you know you don't want to do – he is saying to you that if you are in Christ, if you are found by Him, there are some things you don't have to do. You need not struggle in conflict and confusion: the answer to peace awaits you. In fact, according to Isaiah 9:6, Jesus is the "Prince of Peace!"

You don't need to look for God in all the wrong places. He is saying: "Here I am, looking to be found by you. Don't look to find me at the bottom of an empty brown bottle; don't look to find me in the high of a few snorts of cocaine or that desperate hit of heroin. You will not find me in the painless numbness of a mouth full of pills, because I am life, I am alive. Though it may seem that you are loved by another person, you will not find me in the arms of that someone you have no legal right to be looking for love with." Still, we keep looking – in all the wrong places! Where does this come from? Why are we wandering in the first place?

Early Start on the Wrong Journey

If you don't know Jesus the shepherd, you are lost.

Some of us choose to wander away. Others of us don't even know we are wandering and what it is that we are in search of. Either way, or whatever the condition – we are lost!

Adam and Eve could not have known that their rebelliously impulsive decision to sin would have eternal consequences not just for them, but for every generation that followed. At that particular instant, the desire to taste of a forbidden fruit was much stronger than the desire to obey the command of God, not to eat of it.

In fact, as is true for many of us, the mere fact that we are told not to touch something fixates us on it. The questions that Adam and Eve probably discussed between themselves would have included: Why couldn't they touch it? What might it taste like? How would it affect their lives? Will we really die? What was so special about it anyway? We also ask similar questions as we become increasingly more fixated on the forbidden.

Before long, the thinking shifts to why *not* try it? What can really go wrong? What's wrong with gaining more knowledge and wisdom anyway? Why would God want to keep something good from us? Missing the point completely, we can also easily use the Word of God to rationalize what we want as we start our journey away from God. After all, He states – "*No good thing will he withhold from us –if we walk uprightly*" (Psalms 84:11). Ah, but here's where the problem lies: in rationalizing away our intent to disobey, we begin to move away from walking uprightly, and begin a journey that takes us away from God. The

Word of God does not specify what type of fruit it was; it was, however, quite clear that they were not to eat it or they would suffer the consequence of eating it –death.

"Of every tree of the garden you may freely eat; but of the tree of the knowledge of good and evil you shall not eat, for in the day that you eat of it you shall surely die" (Genesis 2:17).

Eve obviously had some time to consider what God had said, but after consideration, she came to a conclusion that was quite different from what God had declared.

"So when the woman saw that the tree was good for food, that it was pleasant to the eyes, and a tree desirable to make one wise, she took of its fruit and ate. She also gave to her husband with her, and he ate" (Genesis 3:6).

At the end of the day, the kind of fruit was not important. What was of lasting importance was the fact that they ate it when they were told not to. In so doing, they started us all on a journey away from God – a journey that began before we were even born! Yet, out of the moment in the Garden when sin entered into the world, a powerful and divine purpose was born and set in motion. From that moment in the Garden, Jesus was selected to come to earth. His life's purpose? According to Luke 19:10, we learn, *"For the Son of man came to seek and save those who are lost"* (NLT). This is an ongoing and powerfully open invitation for those who are sincerely seeking, searching, wanting to know Christ: Is He for real? Can He really make a difference for me? With all the things that are wrong with me, will He even want me? Those seeking Christ can move through challenges, opposition and barriers because Jesus is waiting on the other side, wanting to be known by them. Jesus even blesses us by drawing us to himself, as Psalm 65:4 declares: *"How blessed is the one you choose, the one you cause to live in your courts. We will be satisfied with the goodness of your house, yes, even with the holiness of your Temple."*

The reality is that we often go about our lives looking for something when all the while it is *someone* that we are looking for. If you seek God but are unwilling to give up your sin, you will not find him because you are seeking him where He is not found.[5] He cannot be found where sin is. If you sincerely desire to let go of your sin, then He will forgive your sin, and you will surely find Him!

Reflection

1. How can our thinking move us in the opposite direction from God?

2. How does moving away from God result in personal conflict and struggles?

Prayer

Lord, help me to turn to you and your way. Thank you for bringing peace in the midst of the situations in my life where I struggle and am pulled in the wrong direction. Amen.

CHAPTER 4

The Right Path

A WAY MUST be found to get back to God. He is looking for us - and we are looking for Him. This is true whether we are aware of it or not. So, let us examine a set of related parables found in Luke chapter 15 in order to understand how much it means to God to find you and to re-connect with Jesus' preferred method of teaching: storytelling. Parables are stories with hidden meanings. Not everyone who hears them can uncover the hidden meaning behind the story. Thus, we can actually relate to the story on a surface level, enjoying it, while missing the entire meaning of the parable. We can miss finding and knowing Jesus in much the same way, even though He is close by and waiting for us. Even Jesus' disciples, who walked with him every day, struggled at times with who Jesus was and what He meant with His words. However, in the Gospels, Jesus always took time to explain what the parables meant. He even began to expect them to know what He meant and who He really was, as in this response to Philip in John 4:19 when Philip asked Him to show them the father: *"Have I been with you all this time, Philip, and yet you still don't know who I am? Anyone who has seen me has seen the Father! So why are you asking me to show him to you?*

But we can also hear the parable and understand the hidden meaning because it is revealed to us by the Holy Spirit. In I Corinthians 4: 12, Paul tells us: *"The person without the Spirit does not accept the things that come from the Spirit of God but considers them foolishness, and cannot understand them because they are discerned only through the Spirit."* It is only then that we can truly understand the full meaning of Jesus's words. Let us now explore the two examples Jesus gave of how far he would go to find you and me.

A Lost Sheep

The story begins with a Shepherd who had 100 sheep, a perfect match and connection to what we were discussing earlier. It was the end of the day and time to close the sheep in for the night. The Shepherd counted the sheep, calling them by name, checking in on them. He got to 99 and thought he was nearly done. But he looked for number 100 and the last sheep was not there. He must have scanned the flock again to see if the sheep was playing and he had simply missed him in the count. But he could not find the sheep. The Bible tells us that the Shepherd locked the 99 sheep in the pen and went out to look for that one single sheep. Yes, the 99 sheep were important but were now safely locked into the fold for the night.

It was dark and night, and who knows how many rocks or hills, how many miles the shepherd had to cover to find that one sheep. He did not know where he had last seen the lost sheep, yet he knew he could not rest that night without the lost sheep safely in the fold. Just so, Jesus left his home in heaven, covered hundreds of millions of miles to come to earth just to die for you and me, to find a way to bring us back to himself. Jesus allowed nothing to dissuade him; nothing changed his mind. It took a tremendous amount of grace (unmerited favor) to find us and bring us back into relationship with him. No wonder the hymn writer puts it this way: *Amazing grace! How sweet the sound that saved a wretch like me! I once was lost but now am found, was blind but now I see.*

He sought the one sheep *until* he found it. It is really important for us to consider the word "until," because it gives us a glimpse of the tenacity and relentless pursuit of the Lord for our relationship, for our love, for our fellowship. It indicates that He would stop at nothing nor allow anything to stop him from winning us back to himself. This gives us such hope! He gave up everything He had so we could have everything He could give – even if He had to give up his life as He did on Calvary nearly 2000 years ago. Matthew says *"if* he finds him" (the sheep). This means there are times when, because of our own will, because of our stubbornness, because we want our own way, even though we hear Him say "Here I am," we still end up turning our backs on all that He has done for us. How sad it is that some of us will simply choose not to come.

Oh, but when that sheep comes home, when he finds that sheep, not only does the Shepherd rejoice, but so does all of heaven. All of the angels are rejoicing with Him over finding that one sheep. If you want to make heaven rejoice, go out and evangelize, get that sheep into the fold, because Jesus came to seek and to save those who were lost. He is more interested in finding that lost sheep than he is concerned about the 99 who are saved and safe. If you do not know Christ, you are important to Him. Important enough for Him to love and give his life for you.

If we are really seeking for God, He will work through our circumstances, through our pain, through problems, through loss, through shattered dreams, and through people around us to bring himself to our attention. Luke goes on to illustrate how to search for God in another example that we can relate to in finding things that are really important to us.

The Lost Coin

You may be asking how do I find Him? How can I get to God? How can I find all I need? There are three ways the parable of the lost coin shows us that might be helpful in answering those questions. The lost coin was of high value to its owner, about a week's wages. In the same way, finding Jesus is something that is priceless! What did the woman who lost the coin do?

First, she lit the lamp. The lamp brings light. Light dispels the darkness. In getting rid of the darkness, things that are hidden in the dark are uncovered. You know the things we may not want others to know about? The things we are ashamed of? Those hidden things are uncovered in the Light.

According to John 1: 4, Jesus is light: *"In him was life and that life was the light of men"* – and if we seek Him and come to Him, His entrance will immediately bring light into our lives. *"The entrance of your word gives light; it gives understanding to the simple"* Psalm 119:130. This light is also about the wisdom, the awareness, the ability to see and discern when things are not right, and the inner knowledge that his word and his presence alone can give us. All benefits that are ours when we find Him!

Second, the woman swept the floor - it's about cleaning out some of the dirt, the cobwebs, the things that the light that is now shining in us brings to our attention. We have to sweep the house clean of the things that would continue to be problems for us is our lives if we do not address them. We have to allow the Lord to make room for his Spirit to work in us – in the temple he will now be living in.

Allow Him to clean the dust out of the corners – it is a cleansing process; several sweeps will be necessary. He wants to make us like himself, so the more we read his Word, the more light comes into our lives to reveal more things that can be uncovered and swept away. It's not about sweeping things under the rug, as we would rather do at times; it's about getting rid of the sin that is uncovered all together. Then we need not be concerned about tripping over that which we have hidden and not dealt with.

Hebrews 12:2 says we are to *"lay aside every weight*

and the sin that so easily besets us." There are some things that we are going to need to get rid of so that God can work in us and in our lives. It's about cleansing us, washing us, and full sanctification. He is willing to cleanse us from our sin – the Word of God can not only uncover the dirt or wrong things in our lives, but it can also wash and cleanse us.

Third, as the woman searched for the coin, even when the lamp was lit, she did not immediately see it; even when she swept the floor, she did not see it at first. In order to come to God (to find Him), you must first believe - Not just with your head, but any realization must drop down 18 inches so you can believe with your heart. You don't want to miss finding Him by just 18 inches! Demons believe and tremble. Human beings believe but do not tremble, and some don't believe in God at all. What I am talking about is not just any kind of belief: it must be belief mixed with faith. You have to have faith to find Jesus, and finding Jesus means that you have found salvation!

Reflection

1. Which of these examples can you best relate to? Sheep? Coin? Why?
2. Will you respond and allow God to light the lamp of your life? More to the point: Will you let him sweep the floor of your life?

Prayer:

Lord, I appreciate you for never giving up on me, for continuing to look for me until you find me. Bring light, cleanse me, and give me faith to believe. Amen

CHAPTER 5

Faith for Finding Jesus

IT TAKES A little faith. Faith activates power – even if it is as small as a mustard seed (Luke 17: 6) - to find all that you need. According to Hebrews 11: 6, *if you are to come to God* (or find Him), *you've got to believe* (your faith) *that He **is** and that He is the rewarder of them that diligently seek Him.* It is this type of faith which gives the hope of eternal life, the reason to go on and live life. Paul says to you: *"If in this life alone we have hope, how miserable we would be among the people"* (I Corinthians 15:19). When you find Jesus, you find hope. Everything changes! Paul puts it this way in Romans 10: 9-10: *"If you confess with your mouth Jesus as Lord, and believe in your heart that God raised Him from the dead, you will be saved; for with the heart a person believes, resulting in righteousness, and with the mouth he confesses, resulting in salvation."* And, this salvation is so great and wonderful that it comes with an eternal hope; a motivation to *"always be ready to give* *a reason for the hope that is within us"* (I Peter 3:15). This, by the way, is how you give your testimony and spread the good news of the Gospel around the world.

So we have to do our part. What an incredibly wonderful promise God gives us! The best thing by far is that when we seek him and turn from doing things our way, there are the extra bonuses of receiving mercy and experiencing pardon for our sins.

Finding and Being Found

I really loved to play the game of hide and seek, and I took pride in not being found. I would hold my breath as the seeker would pass close by so they would not hear or find me. I'm so glad that Jesus does not play the game this way: His game is both serious and intentional.

We are "playing" with life and death. In Jesus' game of hide and seek, He plays to be found. You have to find Him if you are going to live! His invitation to you is: *"Seek ye the Lord while he may be found, call upon him while he is near: Let the wicked forsake his way, and the unrighteous man his thoughts, and let him return unto the Lord, and he will have mercy and He will abundantly pardon"* Isaiah 55:6-7. So, Instead of hiding from you, or keeping himself distant or playing hard to get, because of his love, He pursues so that you can find Him. He shows up in unexpected places and in unexpected people saying, "I am here, will you find me already?"

Satisfied

There is a wonderful story told about a woman, in St.

John chapter four, who kept moving from one partner to the other. By the time we are introduced to her in the story, she had already gone through five men and was working on number six. She was an outcast in her society with no friends: in fact, the other women wanted nothing to do with her. Jesus came to the same well where she had come to get some water.

Jesus was tired and thirsty. He was on a long journey coming from Jerusalem on foot. To save time and energy, he took a shortcut through Samaria. If he were socially correct he would have gone the long way to avoid going through that town. But he had an appointment, at a well, Jacob's well –a convenient oasis for his tired legs and thirsty throat. He had nothing to draw water with. So he sat down, at least to rest. Presently, the woman with her water pot came to the well, to draw water, choosing to come in the middle of the day when no one else would be around. This was highly unusual practice unless she had been spurned, rejected, and avoided enough times to figure that it was less painful to just come for her water when she would be alone. She could not help it that the women did not like her: the men sure did. So the love and acceptance that she was looking for, but could not find in those around her, she sought but had not yet found in her serial relationships with men. Five husbands and counting: At least she married the first five. Now she was working on number six, but she had not yet made up her mind to commit to him in marriage; after all the other five had not worked out.

Today, however, was unusual. There was a man sitting at the well as she approached. She wondered if she should turn around and go back home, but she really needed the water. Maybe she could draw quickly, not say anything and quickly head back home. There was no one else around. The man sitting at the well looked like he was tired. Maybe he would remain quiet in keeping with the custom? She pressed forward.

Little did she know that this encounter would be so life-changing. The man broke with convention and asked her for water. She raised the conventional issues with his request such as Jews don't talk to Samaritans, how could you ask me for water, do you know who I am? He responded: if you know who I am, you would ask me for living water. Oh, and by the way, I know you have already gone through five failed marriages, and the man you are with right now is not your husband. Jesus was saying to her I know you have been seeking inner spiritual satisfaction in the relationships you have had, but you have not found it. But, *I know the plans I have for you plans of good and not of evil to give you a future and a hope. Then you will call upon me and I will answer you - If you seek me you will surely find me if you seek me with all your heart."* Jeremiah 29:11-12. In other words, "*the water I give …will become in [you] a spring of water welling up into everlasting life."* John 4:14. Jesus was letting her know that she had finally found what she had been looking for, and offering her a brand new way of life. It was an offer she could not refuse. Jesus offered her living water, gave her new courage, fresh boldness, with such electrifying power that she forgot about her water pot, and her inhibitions, and ran into the city with a brand new life and message for all: Come see the man who gave me a life worth living!

As we are looking for Him, he has also been looking for us. He is near to you right now. He is in this place right here, right now, speaking to us about our future and the plans he has for us. This is what you are looking for; this is how you can find all you need.

If the person being sought does not want to be found, then the seeker will look and look and look but they may never find the one they are seeking. What a hopeless situation if you love them! But when Jesus is in the picture, he places himself near enough for us to find Him. He gives us clues, and opportunities like in John 3: 16, where He tells us: *"For God so loved the world that he gave his one and only Son, that whoever believes in him shall not perish but have eternal life."* He tugs at our heart, and He shows up in our lives in unmistakable appearances. He will allow himself to be found by us. Hallelujah!

I am so excited by this kind of God!

The efforts of the woman at the well were not in vain: she shared her exciting experience with her entire village. The efforts of the woman who had lost the coin were also not in vain – she found her coin and began to rejoice. She shared and celebrated with her friends! Much like the angels rejoiced in heaven over the lost sheep, so her friends rejoiced with her over the lost coin. We too will rejoice with you when you come to the Lord because you *will* find Him.

How do I find What I Need?

Finding what you need requires a stop at the cross-roads of the cross. What that means is that the cross is the place where Jesus gave his life for you and me in the single most phenomenal expression of love that has ever been recorded in history. At the beginning of this book, I stated that his purpose for coming was to seek and to save those who were lost. John 3:16 tells us how he did it. So Jesus the Son of God came to earth as the son of man. He took on the form of a human being and limited himself to the confines of a little baby's body. Imagine this for a moment: the creator of the universe in a baby's body, totally dependent on a woman he had created to take care of his every need. But it didn't stop there. After all, a baby cannot do much saving. We are told in Luke 2:52 *"And Jesus grew in wisdom and stature and in favor with God and man"*. And we know that he as an adult went around talking about his kingdom that was coming, correcting and teaching everyone who was willing to hear what He had to say. He performed miracles of healing: blood conditions, blindness, speaking, fevers. He cast out demons, restored people to their right minds. He raised people from the dead. He turned water into wine saving a wedding from failure.

What He Did for Us

But the time came when He had to fulfill the purpose for which he had been born on Earth. He came to die. And He began a journey on the road to Calvary that took him through the last supper with the disciple who would betray him, to the garden of Gethsemane where even his closest disciples could not stay awake to pray with Him at his toughest moment.

On the journey, he replaced the ear for a soldier that Peter cut off defending him; he was captured by the High priests and sold out by Judas for 30 pieces of silver. The same Peter who defended him so vigorously with the sword denied he ever knew Him —not just once but three times! The journey also took him through a mocking, jeering crowd, an unjust and rigged trial that found him guilty of wrong (sins) that he never committed.

He endured a terrible beating and was sentenced to die on the cross. In his weakened physical state, He was forced to carry the cross on which He would hang until He could carry it no more. After He reached the hill Golgotha, they nailed him to the cross of Calvary. There he hung, like a bridge suspended between us and God; his outstretched arms including the whole world. The ultimate example of love and reconciliation and access to a holy God we would otherwise never be able to connect to. It was at the cross that *"… God made Christ, who never sinned, to be the offering for our sin, so that we could be made right with God through Christ."* (2 Corinthians 5:21). What a wonderfully marvelous thought! But this is the important point of this book: it is here that something must be done by each of us.

Decision Point

Yes, here is where the decision point is reached: what are you going to do about the life He gave? Are you going to choose to find Him or remain in the lost and found of life? He gave his life for you, and for me – for the whole world! When He gave his life, He took our sins and the punishment that we deserved. He provided forgiveness for the sins of the world and paid in full the price that we would ordinarily have to pay, and then He provided us the gift of eternal life. He came to the lost and found to re-claim *you*. Deciding to take, or receive, the forgiveness of sins and the gift Jesus provided is how you are saved, born again as a child of God, AND how you find all you need. Because all you need is found in Jesus!

Which way will you take? Will you accept the gift of forgiveness and eternal life? He promises: *"Therefore, if anyone is in Christ, he is a new creation. The old has passed away; behold, the new has come."* 2 Corinthians 5:17. Of all the choices you can make in life, this will be the most important one; the one with the greatest life-changing ef-fect, because you will be born again and he will make you into a new creation.

So at the crossroads of your life you can find Him. At the lost and found of your life –He came to reclaim you. Instead of trying this way, that way, or another way you can find Jesus – the only way to the life you have always wanted: A life worth living! Now that you know how to find and be found by Him, I can begin to describe what happens when you find Jesus.

Reflection

1. How is Finding Jesus a matter of Life and Death?
2. Are you going to choose to find him, or remain in the 'lost and found' of life?

Prayer

Lord, thank you for taking me out of the lost and found, and providing me with a place where I will forever belong. Amen.

CHAPTER 6

A Life Worth Living

WHAT HAPPENS WHEN we find Him? There is something about finding Jesus that can be difficult to express, but I will not miss this opportunity to share some of the things that are included in the wonderful, unforgettable, life-changing experience of finding Jesus. I can start by saying that we fit together like a 'hand in a glove,' that we take to Him like a 'duck to water,' that we have come 'home to roost;' all common expressions for saying that we have finally found the place where we belong. These are all colloquial expressions that let us know that He is exactly what we have been looking for all our lives.

But there's more to it than that. Like David, we can say – *"Oh taste and see that the Lord is good –blessed is the man that trusts in him"* (Psalm 34:8). We can say like the songwriter, "Hallelujah, I have found him, whom my soul so long has craved. Jesus satisfies my longing through his blood I now am saved."[4]

If you are seeking something today, if you've been looking for love in all the wrong places, I am here to tell you that He knows all about it and we could never find what we are looking for without Him. And as the good shepherd, He gave his life for the sheep.

The way has already been made; the price has already been paid. And though it cost Him everything (*The wages of sin is death* - Romans 6:23a), Jesus gives it to us as a gift (*the gift of God is eternal life through Jesus Christ the Lord* - Romans 6:23b); Then He goes beyond that and gives us the power to receive the gift. John 1:12 declares: "*But as many as received him to them he gave the power to become the sons of God –even to them that believe on his name.*" Is this awesome or what? If we try to rationalize it, we will come up short because our finite minds cannot fathom the ways or thoughts of an infinite God. But God knows that some of us are very logically minded, and he offers to reason or discuss the matter with us in Isaiah 1:18 where he invites you to "*come now, let us settle the matter,*" says the LORD. "*Though your sins are like scarlet, they shall be as white as snow; though they are red as crimson, they shall be like wool...*" So let us think it through and discuss it together as we answer the question:

What happens when we find Jesus?

The Psalmist David points out: '*My soul finds rest in God alone; my salvation comes from him*' (Psalm 62:1). St Augustine confesses: "Thou hast made us for thyself, O Lord, and our heart is restless until it finds its rest in thee."[3] Thus, finding Jesus is finding someone that has a name that is above every other name. Solomon declares: *"The name of the Lord is a strong tower; the righteous run into it and are safe"* (Proverbs 18:10).

This is experiential proof positive that the name of the Lord is not just any name, but a name that embodies the many things we need Him to be all at the same time. For example, if you are looking for peace, run into his name – *He is Prince of Peace* (Isaiah 9:6). If you are looking for love, run into his name – *God is love* (I John 4:8). Are you sick and in need of healing? Run into his name – He is the *Lord your healer* (Exodus 15:26). If you are in need of provision, run into his name – He is *Jehovah Jireh, the one who provides* (Genesis 22:14). Whatever the situation, run into his name – because He is the God of more than enough! You will find in Him whatever you need. All of his nature, essence, and characteristics are bound up in his name: a thorough discussion would take another entire book. But if you do a study of all of the names of God, you are in for quite an eye-opener as you begin to understand the treasure of who it really is that you have found!

When you find Jesus, you find the one called the Shepherd and Bishop of your soul. The one to whom you can hand things over. There are going to be some rough and dangerous places to walk through in your life, where it may seem that your very life is threatened. But He will see you through thick and thin, because of who He is.

It is only fitting that we cap things off by going back for a moment to Psalms 23: *verse 1 The Lord is my Shepherd and I shall not* want, is the ultimate statement in terms of protection and safety that is possible once God is truly in charge of our lives. He will satisfy our every need to the extent that we will not want for anything. For example, we will be at peace as he provides for us a place of abundance in verse 2:

He makes me to lie down in green pastures.

No dry places, no dead places, just life in places of abundance and beauty. Then God ensures that we have the ability to drink for our refreshment and restores us when we are weary and in need of revival. You see, sheep do not drink water if it is rough and swirling. They will, however, drink if the water is still. It is also difficult for us to stop and drink if the water is rough, therefore we will not get to feel refreshed because we will not be able to drink and quench our thirst. So in verse 3 David confirms that *He leads me beside still waters, He restores my soul.* After we have rested and refreshed ourselves, we can say that we are revived, rested and restored.

But God does not leave it there. He does so much more for his beloved children, for those who find Him. For example, on our life's journey we can depend on Him to *lead* [us] *in the paths of righteousness for his name's sake.*

He takes purposeful time out to teach us his will and way. He shows us what is right. He instructs us in his laws, teaches us the way we should go, what to do to please Him, and how to walk in a way that honors Him. Since our *righteousness is like filthy rags in his sight* (Isaiah 64:6), we have no real choice other than to put on (dress ourselves in) the righteousness of God's son Jesus – his name sake.

So by the time we get to verse 4, *yea, though I walk through the valley of the shadow of death,* the Lord is communicating quite clearly that there are going to be some rough and dangerous places to walk through, where it may seem that our very lives are threatened. But with Him as shepherd, guide, and protector, fear need not be a major factor: *I will fear no evil, for thou art with me!* His presence alone calms our fear, makes us feel safe and invincible in the presence of his omnipotence.

Thy rod and staff they comfort me. Like sheep need someone to look out for their safety, to comfort and correct them, to protect them from wild animals and even from themselves, so also we need someone – a Shepherd – to pull us back from self-destruction or from the dangerous places we would surely end up if left to our own devices.

With God as our Shepherd, the fact that we have enemies will not deter us from receiving and living out our blessings according to verse 5: *You prepare a table before me in the presence of my enemies.* Oh yes, even in the presence of your enemies, what God has for you will be for you, even if others don't want you to have it. If God wants you to have it, you will have it. No devil in hell can stop it from happening in the fullness of time. Whom God has blessed is blessed forever!

You anoint my head with oil; my cup overflows. The oil symbolizes the anointing of the Holy Spirit. His power in us, like the oil does for the sheep, serves to keep the pests away from us. Much like pests or flies will prevent sheep from resting, so the distractions and irritations of life can hinder us from being fully at peace, or from being able to rest were it not for the anointing of the Holy Spirit on our lives. Perhaps you are dealing with irritations, distractions and frustrations in your life right now that seem like they are not going away anytime soon. I recommend looking to the Holy Spirit and his fruit (oil) in our lives to combat these negative influences. His *love, joy, peace, patience gentleness goodness, meekness, and self-control* (Galatians 5: 22-23) are quite a solid prescription for these persistent ailments.

When we are at rest, what overflowing blessings and peace are actually ours to enjoy! David rejoices as he concludes in verse 6: *Surely goodness and mercy will follow me all the days of my life, and I will dwell in the house of the Lord forever.* The promise of goodness and mercy can be fulfilled because God is good, and He is merciful –and He is with us. Since He will never leave us or forsake us, his goodness and mercy are with us always. Whenever we look around, there they are!

When you find Jesus, you find the one who will stand *guard* over you all the days of your life because SURELY his *goodness*, on one side, is following you so that everything will work together for your good because you love God. Then, on the other side, He sets up his mercy. His mercy will follow us whenever we need it. In fact, He tells us that if we need more mercy, we can *"… come boldly to the throne of our gracious God. There we will receive his mercy, and we will find grace to help us when we need it most"* (Hebrews 4:16, NLT): when our supply is low or when we are fresh out.

When you find Jesus, you find the one with whom you will dwell forever (John 14:6) because he has gone to prepare a place for you and will come again to receive you to himself. Then, the promise of living with Him for eternity puts the proverbial icing on the cake. No matter what you may be facing right now, even after goodness and mercy have followed us through life, to know that we will end up living with Him forever makes all the challenges worth it.

Wait – Just a little More!

When you find Jesus, you find salvation –salvation from the power of sin, the guilt of sin! You also find forgiveness for every sin you have ever committed. You find life, you find the way, you find the truth to counter all the lies you have been told or might even have begun to believe. You find the bread of life for your hungry soul. You find a river of living water to satisfy your thirst. You find the One who loves you unconditionally – even if nobody else loves you. You find the only person who can take a nobody like me and change me into somebody like Him.

When you find Jesus, you find the only one who has been longing to take you on – even with the imperfect life you may be sick and tired of. That will not deter Him – He will take you on with all your imperfections and transform you into a new creation! He is the only one who can make you into everything that God intended for you to be. If Jesus offers you all of this when you have found Him, why would you look for another?

A Door and A Way

When you find Jesus, you also find the Door. He says of himself: *"I am the door: by me if anyone enters in, he shall be saved, and shall go in and out, and find pasture"* (John 10:9, KJV). We already saw that *He is the way* (John 14:6), the only way to God. Here's where some of us get stuck... Not many find this path because it is a narrow way. According to Matthew 7:13-14, *"Narrow is the way that leads to life and few there be that find it."* The narrowness is understandable because Jesus is the Door. We must enter through Him. So when He finds you, you find the way to God. When He died on Calvary, the veil of the temple, separating us from what was usually reserved for the priests alone, was torn in two, providing permanent and direct access to God. Can you now begin to see why some people never find it? Some are looking for another way, a way that is more pleasing to their preferences, one that provides more variety. Those who never find the way remain in the Lost and Found of life, forever waiting to be picked up by their owner. Though He paid the price for them, they never connect with Him and will spend their lives wandering. You can choose today to come to Him, to be found by Him. You can choose today to seek Him with all your heart because you will surely find Him. You can, together with Him, come out of the Lost and Found of life! And, it is because of His amazing grace that we even have this opportunity to finally live a full and satisfying life.

The poem *"The Hound of Heaven"*[1] expresses this journey in olde English. The familiar hymn "Satisfied"[4] expresses the same journey in language we can clearly understand:

All my life long I had panted
For a draught from some cool spring,
That I hoped would quench the burning
Of the thirst I felt within.

Hallelujah! I have found Him
Whom my soul so long has craved!
Jesus satisfies my longings;
Through His life I now am saved.

Well of water, ever springing,
Bread of life, so rich and free,
Untold wealth that never faileth,
My Redeemer is to me.

Clara T. Williams (1875)[4].

Reflection

1. Which of the benefits of finding Jesus is most important to you today?
2. Which one(s) do you still need to receive from Jesus?

Prayer

Lord, Thank you so much for coming to seek me, and for finding me. I receive you, and all the benefits that you bring into my life right now. Because you supply all that I need according to your riches in glory in Christ Jesus, My life is now worth living. Amen.

Because He is close, we can draw near. Seek Him for yourself. Look for Him; reach for Him: You will surely find Him! If you find Jesus, or want to know how, as a result of reading this booklet, contact us and let us know.

End Notes

[1]Thompson, F. (1893). The Hound of Heaven. Poems.

[2]Scriptures taken from The King James Version®, unless otherwise specified.

[3]Saint Augustine, Confessions, trans. Henry Chadwick. Oxford, Oxford University Press, 2008.

[4]Williams, C.T. (1875). Satisfied. Public Domain

[5]Guyon, M. (2014). A Short method of Prayer. Book Three. Reprint In A Classic Collection of Prayer. (p. 276). Christian Art Publishers.

CPSIA information can be obtained
at www.ICGtesting.com
Printed in the USA
LVOW04*0521010116
467822LV00006BC/20/P

9 780986 211102